SPOTLIGHT ON THE RISE AND FALL OF ANCIENT CIVILIZATIONS™

ANCIENT MESOPOTAMIAN TECHNOLOGY

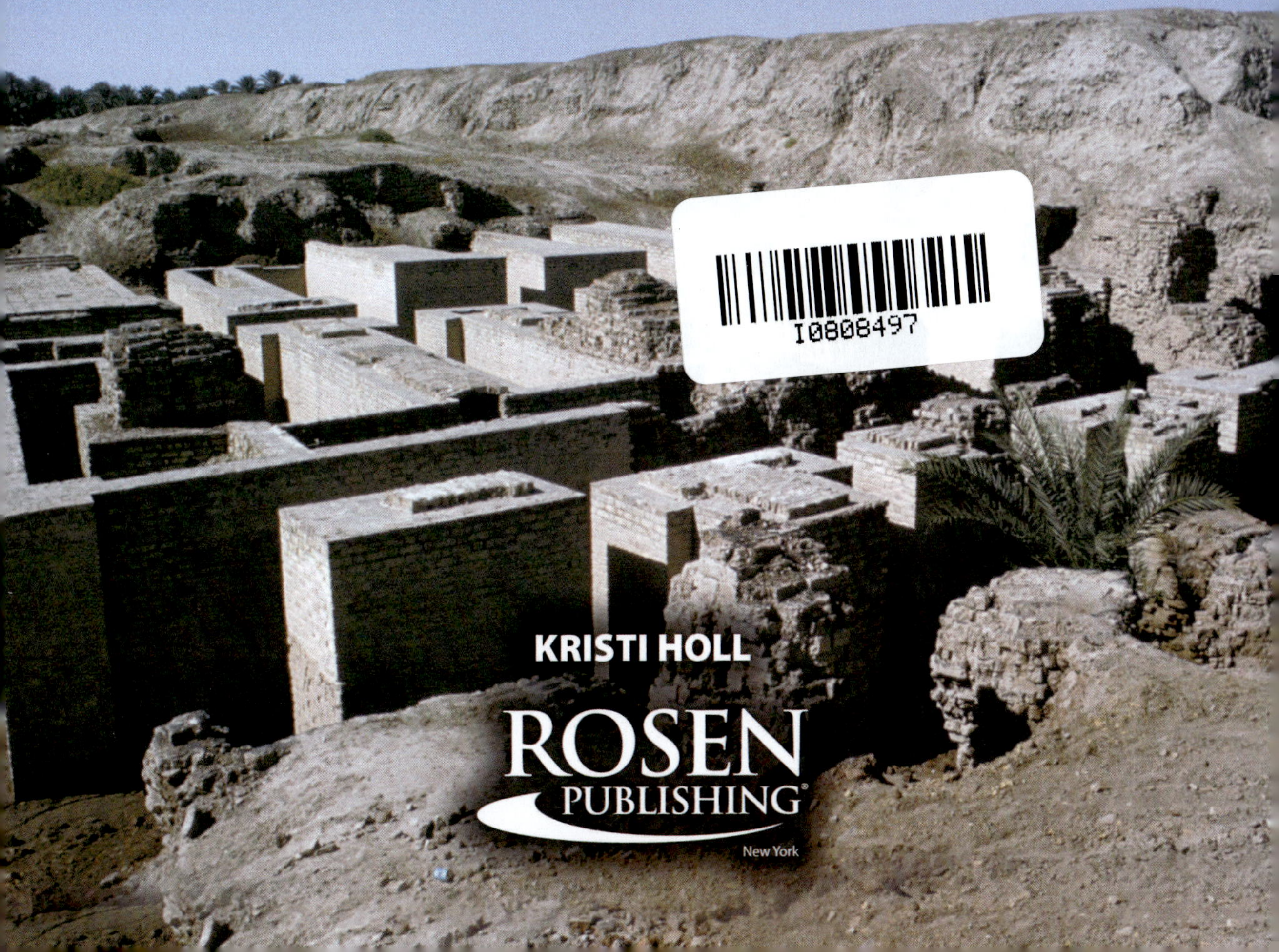

KRISTI HOLL

ROSEN PUBLISHING
New York

Published in 2017 by The Rosen Publishing Group, Inc.
29 East 21st Street, New York, NY 10010

First Edition

Library of Congress Cataloging-in-Publication Data

Names: Holl, Kristi.
Title: Ancient Mesopotamian technology / Kristi Holl.
Description: New York : Rosen Publishing, 2017. | Series: Spotlight on the rise and fall of ancient civilizations | Audience: Grades 7–12. | Includes bibliographical references and index.
Identifiers: LCCN 2016003633| ISBN 9781499438109 (library bound) | ISBN 9781477789537 (pbk.) | ISBN 9781477789483 (6-pack)
Subjects: LCSH: Technology—Iraq—History—To 634—Juvenile literature. | Iraq—Civilization—To 634—Juvenile literature. | Iraq—History—To 634—Juvenile literature.
Classification: LCC T16 .H65 2017 | DDC 609.35—dc23
LC record available at http://lccn.loc.gov/2016003633

Manufactured in the United States of America

CONTENTS

LAND BETWEEN THE RIVERS	4
WATER SUPPLY: CANALS, IRRIGATION, AND AQUEDUCTS	6
CHALLENGES OF FOOD PRODUCTION	8
WEAVING	10
POTTERY AND ITS MANY USES	12
THE WHEEL	14
METALS AND METALWORKING	16
CRAFTSMEN: GLASS, STONE, AND JEWELS	18
CONSTRUCTION MATERIALS	20
ARRANGEMENT OF HOMES	22
BUILDING CITIES	24
ZIGGURATS	26
ON THE MOVE IN MESOPOTAMIA	28
MATHEMATICS, WEIGHTS, AND MEASURES	30
ASTRONOMY AND ASTROLOGY	32
TREATING THE SICK	34
ADVANCES IN WARFARE	36
THE FIRST WRITERS	38
GIFTS FROM THE CRADLE OF CIVILIZATION	40
GLOSSARY	42
FOR MORE INFORMATION	43
FOR FURTHER READING	45
BIBLIOGRAPHY	46
INDEX	47

LAND BETWEEN THE RIVERS

Ancient Mesopotamia is often called the "cradle of civilization." Wandering nomads began grouping together in villages, then cities. They turned a farming population into the world's first urban society. People began to work together. Many inventions came from this area, such as writing and the wheel. They invented accounting and used astronomy to develop a calendar.

The Mesopotamians used technology to improve their everyday lives. The word "technology" comes from two Greek words. *Techne* means "art" or "craft," and *logos* means "word" or "study." Technology means to use scientific study and craftsmanship to perform jobs.

There was no single country called Mesopotamia. The name describes the land between the Tigris and Euphrates Rivers. Today, it includes the countries of Iraq and parts of Syria, Turkey, and Iran. Ancient Mesopotamia consisted of different city-states that rose and fell. In approximate order, these city-states included Ur and Uruk, Sumer, Akkad, Babylon, and Assyria.

Ancient Mesopotamia never existed as a separate country. Mesopotamia describes the area in the Middle East that lies primarily between two rivers, the Tigris and Euphrates.

WATER SUPPLY: CANALS, IRRIGATION, AND AQUEDUCTS

Nearly every spring, from March through June, the Tigris and Euphrates Rivers overflowed. This enriched the soil. However, sometimes floods washed away whole villages. Men tried to build dams to control the rivers. These barriers eroded quickly because of their soft soil. Some years the floods didn't happen at all. This was difficult for the people, too. Those in the desert counted on the floodwaters for many things, so Mesopotamians invented ways to save and move water. They needed a sure supply for drinking, cooking, plumbing, and irrigating crops.

After the floodwaters receded, the flat lands between the rivers left swamps. So the people built underground aqueducts. They transported water across northern Mesopotamia through underground channels. They also dug canals and drained the swamp water into canals for storage. The importance of canals is shown in a Mesopotamian curse. It says, "May your canal become choked with debris!"

Growing populations needed water, but sometimes there was no river nearby. Water for drinking and crops was transported to them over long distances through aqueducts.

CHALLENGES OF FOOD PRODUCTION

Early Mesopotamians only farmed in areas near hills. Enough rain fell there to grow crops. The region supported the growth of wheat, barley, and wild cereals. Farmers used hoes to prepare the ground. Planting seeds required digging a hole or long furrow in the soil to receive the seeds.

By 5800 BCE, people lived in the southern plains of the Tigris and Euphrates Rivers. The land in this region was extremely fertile. However, there wasn't enough rainfall here to grow crops. They could carry water from the rivers for their plants, but the rivers sometimes dried up during hot summers when water was needed most.

Irrigation and the invention of the plow around 3500 BCE transformed agriculture. With irrigation farmers could grow crops on the level plains. Their first plow was simply a sharp-edged stone attached to a wooden shaft and pulled by oxen. It was primitive, but it made increased production possible.

Most farmers made tools from locally available clay, stone, and timber. Farm tools were needed to prepare the ground, plant the seeds, and harvest the crop.

WEAVING

Looms for weaving fabric appeared early in the third millennium. Sumerian clay tablets from around 2200 BCE described a growing weaving business. The need for cloth was great in the palace and temple, so hundreds of women were hired to weave. At first weaving took place only in homes, but that changed around 2100 BCE. Weaving factories in Ur and Lagash gave jobs to women and girls in the city. Six hundred years later, smaller numbers of men were also employed as weavers.

Cloth was made from several different materials. Wool from sheep and goats was the most common fabric used to make clothing. Wool was made into many types of garments, from cloaks to shoes. Linen was a more deluxe fabric. Linen was woven for the wealthy families and the priests. It was also used to adorn statues of gods. Later, Mesopotamian weavers imported other materials like cotton and silk for their creations.

Wool was often made into ***kaunakes***, or woven woolen skirts or cloaks, worn around 2500 BCE. These kaunakes replaced sheepskin.

POTTERY AND ITS MANY USES

Ancient Mesopotamians often made pottery in their homes. Pots were created by hand using several methods. People made coil pots by rolling long clay "snakes"; the pot's sides were then built by spiraling the snakes upward. Slab pots started with a flat clay "pancake" as a base with flat slabs added for sides. Workers made pinch pots by first pushing a thumb into a ball of clay; they used thumbs and index fingers to pinch and pull the clay upward.

Around 3500 BCE the Uruk culture began mass-producing pottery on a potter's wheel. Clay was made into cups, plates, and pots. The production of pottery then moved from the household into the hands of skilled craftsmen. Pottery was used for preserving and storing food, such as grain, oil, beer, water, and wine. Artisans created designs in the clay pieces using metal tools, shells, teeth, bone, rocks, and sharpened sticks.

Clay could be shaped by hand or on a potter's wheel, then hardened, glazed, and painted. The shape and size give clues as to how the pot was used.

THE WHEEL

The first wheels invented around 3500 BCE weren't used for transportation. Instead, the first wheel served as a potter's wheel. Later the Sumerians didn't simply turn a potter's wheel on end and attach it to a wagon. Instead, the wheel went through many stages of development over three hundred years. Then it was used on chariots and wagons for moving heavy objects from one location to another. It's believed that several cultures adapted the wheel independently during this time.

The first wheels were man-made logs. Long planks were attached to each other. Then the stack of planks was fashioned into a log. These "logs" were placed under sledges. As the sledges were moved forward, the log in back was moved to the front.

The next stage was the wheel-axle combination. Two flat wheels without spokes were connected by an axle. Even with better wheels, camels were a more efficient form of transportation in the desert.

This carved stone picture (called a relief) was found in the palace of Sennacherib. It shows the king riding in a chariot on wheels.

METALS AND METALWORKING

Mesopotamians first worked with metal as primary ores such as gold, silver, and copper. (Ore is mined because it contains a useful material, such as a metal or coal.) Gold and silver were flexible and would flatten when hammered, which made it easy for ancient man to shape and use the materials. Gold and silver were valued and used mostly as jewelry. However, neither ore was hard enough to be used for weapons or tools.

Copper was soft enough to be shaped into objects without heating it. However, copper was improved by mixing it with other metals. Copper combined with tin produced bronze. Bronze was easier to cast in molds than copper. The finished objects were also much harder than copper and as strong as some steel. Bronze was used in a wide variety of things. They made bronze axes, hammers, sickles, daggers, and swords. During the fourth millennium BCE, farm tools and weapons were made of bronze.

Ancient Mesopotamian cultures practiced surgery to some degree, using small copper knives and bronze lancets (sharp-pointed two-edged instruments) for making small incisions.

CRAFTSMEN: GLASS, STONE, AND JEWELS

Mesopotamian craftsmen invented glass around 1600 BCE. Glass vessels were molded around a core shape. First, liquid glass was poured over a clay center. The glass was allowed to cool and become solid. The clay was later scraped out. Craftsmen used glass to make containers, beads, small figures, and parts of statues.

Other craftsmen included bronze workers, silversmiths, and goldsmiths. They made objects out of stone, metal, and jewels. Gold was used to make necklaces and other jewelry. It was also made into daggers, helmets, and statues of gods and goddesses. Jewelry was often decorated with stones such as agate or jasper.

The Mesopotamians were skilled stone carvers. They carved statues of their gods and goddesses out of marble and limestone. The Assyrians also carved stone pictures called reliefs for their palaces. The reliefs included hunting scenes and battle scenes. Statues and stone reliefs were decorated with gems.

This cylinder was discovered in the royal tomb of Ur in Mesopotamia. The finished glass vessel is decorated with gold and quartz.

CONSTRUCTION MATERIALS

Mesopotamian building materials included reeds, wood, stone, and mud bricks. Reeds were plentiful and harvested along the banks of the Tigris and Euphrates Rivers. Reeds were commonly used because that meant houses could be built quickly and cheaply. Very little wood was available for construction, so people had to be inventive. Large stones were saved for more important buildings than houses.

Mud was also an abundant construction material. Many Mesopotamians lived in mud brick houses that were sealed and waterproofed with tar. The bricks were made from river mud. Clay mixed with sand or finely chopped straw was stronger. The best time to make sun-dried bricks was during the hot summer. In fact, the first month of summer was called "the month of bricks." Some mud bricks were fired or baked in kilns. This made bricks harder and longer lasting. However, baked bricks were more expensive to produce because the wood needed for fueling the kilns was scarce.

This model of an early brick house shows walls of mud blocks, made of clay mixed with straw. The roof was probably constructed from branches and mud.

ARRANGEMENT OF HOMES

Whether rich or poor, every family had its own house. Near the rivers, people built round or rectangular reed houses, with a roof of woven reeds. After cities developed, sunbaked mud bricks were used. These mud brick houses were more permanent and larger than the reed dwellings. Sun-dried bricks were used in many parts of Mesopotamia. They required thick walls and small doors to ensure durability. Bricks allowed to stay damp would crumble, so a system of tiny canals was drilled into the walls for rainwater drainage.

Rooms were often built around a center court for privacy and safety. Meals could be cooked in the center court. Children played there, and small livestock was kept there. Courtyards kept things cooler during blistering summer heat. Thick brick walls absorbed heat slowly, remaining relatively cool. Upper floors were where the family lived. During good weather, people would cook and eat on the flat roof.

Whether in the average Mesopotamian home or in a palace, walls surrounding center courts provided both privacy and safety from intruders. Much activity of daily living took place here.

BUILDING CITIES

The first small city-states appeared in the fourth millennium. They grew between the Euphrates and Tigris Rivers. The rivers provided plenty of water for farming, so people moved to the open plains. But the flat ground left them vulnerable, which led to many invasions. They were conquered by other people. The building of walled cities likely occurred for protection.

Cities may also have grown as a result of the environment. Low rainfall might have been one reason people grouped themselves together. It took many men working together to build irrigation canals.

This was a unique time in history. Humans were working together to meet community needs. And cities grew! Around 2700 BCE, the city of Uruk was enclosed by a high brick wall. Inside were roughly one hundred thousand people. By 600 BCE, the city of Babylon had two hundred thousand people. Its protective wall around the city measured 10 miles (16 kilometers).

This aerial view of the archaeological site of Uruk, built by the famous Sumerian king Gilgamesh, clearly shows the walls that first made the city well known.

ZIGGURATS

Ancient Sumerians believed powerful gods lived in the sky. They built tall structures called ziggurats to reach the heavens. Historians believe that temples were built on top of the ziggurats. (However, no temple has ever been found.) Ziggurats were built in a series of rectangular tiers, or platforms. Each platform was smaller than the one below it. Ramps similar to staircases were built to climb from one platform up to the next. The Egyptians later copied this design for their pyramids.

A ziggurat's interior was built of sun-dried bricks. The outside, however, needed to be waterproof. It was constructed of bricks baked in a kiln, then filled in with bitumen mortar. (The mortar was made from oil that seeped out of the ground.) Thick layers of reed matting were stuffed in the layers of interior brickwork to make it stronger. The best preserved Mesopotamian ziggurat today is in Ur, dating from around 2000 BCE.

Worshippers climbed the Ziggurat of Ur using ramps that resembled stair steps. They reached the temple at the top using these ramps to climb from one level to the next.

ON THE MOVE IN MESOPOTAMIA

For short distances, many in Mesopotamia walked or rode oxen. The most common way to travel longer distances was by water, on the rivers or on the canals. Both the Tigris and Euphrates Rivers flow from north to south, and many boats carried cargo south on the rivers.

A boat called a *quppu* could be paddled. It was a circular basket covered with animal hides. Rafts called *kalakkus* were also used. They were made from reeds laid on top of inflated goat skins. For sea journeys (in the Red Sea, Indian Ocean, and Persian Gulf) Sumerians built boats out of wood. Even today, Marsh Arabs in Iraq still use boats made from waterproofed reeds.

Where there was no water, goods were also dragged across the ground on sleds, or sledges. It was easier than pulling a wheeled cart over desert sand. These sleds transported heavy loads like rocks, rather than people.

Travel by water, on river or canal, was a common way to make a journey in ancient Mesopotamia. This carved stone relief was found in Kalhu, now northern Iraq.

MATHEMATICS, WEIGHTS, AND MEASURES

Ancient Mesopotamians needed to count and measure things. So they invented basic mathematics. This was at least 1,500 years before anyone else. They started by using a person's ten fingers for counting. Our base ten number system, or decimal system, came from this. They also invented a base sixty system. It was first used with weights. (A load weighing 67 pounds [30 kilograms] was called a talent. The talent was divided into sixty *minas*, and each mina equaled sixty *shekels*.)

Length was measured with the cubit, which was 20 inches (50 centimeters). The Babylonian mile was 6 miles (almost 10 km) longer than our modern mile. Their farmland was measured by a unit called a field, which was a bit smaller than 1 acre (.40 hectares).

Clay tablets proved that they also knew about geometry. They wrote down the formula to figure lengths of a right triangle's sides. This was a thousand years before Pythagoras, who was famous for this discovery!

This piece of tablet dates from the second millennium BCE Babylonian civilization. It clearly shows square and triangular geometric shapes.

ASTRONOMY AND ASTROLOGY

Ancient Mesopotamians also needed to keep track of time. They had to know when to plant and harvest. They also needed to predict the arrival of the yearly floods. Time was needed to move to safety. Mesopotamians tracked the passage of time by studying the sky. The changing positions of the stars, planets, and moon were noted. They worshipped the sun god Shamash and the moon god Sin. Mesopotamians believed that the gods moved the sun, moon, planets, and stars through the sky.

The Sumerians designed a calendar of twelve months like we use today. Each month began when a new crescent moon was spotted. The Sumerians also invented the zodiac. This divided circles into twelve equal parts, one for each sign. Each sign of the zodiac represented a constellation. Mesopotamians also divided days into twenty-four hours. They constantly searched the heavens for unusual events like comets and eclipses.

This astrological calendar from the Sumerian city of Uruk is divided into twelve months. Based on studies of the sky, it was used to determine times for planting and harvesting.

TREATING THE SICK

More than thirty thousand clay tablets covered with cuneiform symbols describe Mesopotamian medical practices. Two types of healers treated their sick. An *asu* was an herbalist doctor. He was often found in a special room in the temple. The asu kept jars of medicines on hand. Some contained dried leaves or powders made from ground seeds. Others held pieces of tree bark and mixtures made with plant and animal fat. The herbs were mixed with milk or date honey to disguise the bitter taste. Sometimes asus also performed surgery.

It was also believed that sins caused some diseases—that an evil spirit could enter a person. So sometimes the *ashipu* healer was called. (He was also referred to as a sorcerer.) He knew the spells for praying to the right gods to get rid of evil spirits. This was important, people felt, because then the demon couldn't spread the disease, going from one family member into another.

Found in Nineveh, this clay cuneiform tablet contains written medical prescriptions. They include directions to the chemist and directions for the patient's use of the medicine.

ADVANCES IN WARFARE

Mesopotamian kings built huge empires for several reasons. They felt safer when the city-state was larger. Kings also went to war for financial gain. They taxed the people they conquered and took prisoners for slave labor. Two city-states, Lagash and Umma, fought the first recorded war around 2500 BCE. Within two hundred years, military force was used on a massive scale against any city that stood in a king's way.

There were two types of soldiers. Light infantrymen wore no armor. They wielded long spears for stabbing, not throwing. They also carried battle-axes for slashing through helmets. Heavy infantrymen, however, wore armor and helmets. They stood in closely packed ranks; each man held up a large shield. Their spears projected through the spaces between the shields. Battlewagons were too cumbersome to use for fighting. Wheel technology advanced later (2000 to 1595 BCE). This enabled soldiers to launch attacks from chariots.

This artwork depicting Sumerian soldiers was discovered in a royal tomb at Ur from about 2600 to 2400 BCE. Its tile pieces include shells, red limestone, and lapis lazuli laid on coal.

THE FIRST WRITERS

Perhaps the greatest development the Mesopotamians gave us was writing. The Sumerians developed writing between 3500 and 3300 BCE. The first writers were called scribes. This special class of people was trained to read and write. Scribes pressed pointed sticks, bones, or reeds into moist clay tablets. Then the tablets dried and hardened. These tablets became the world's first letters, account sheets, and books.

Early writing changed over time from small pictures to tiny marks. The marks were arranged in many groups called cuneiform. This means "wedge shaped." The scribes used nearly six hundred separate cuneiform signs, so reading and writing the language was very difficult.

Many of the clay tablets contain business and trading records. Others record fables, songs, and poems. Medical practices and mathematical formulas were written down. So were long lists of local plants and animals. The early tablets are extremely valuable. They truly capture the Mesopotamian culture.

This cuneiform tablet describes one of the three most powerful Mesopotamian gods, Enki. He was believed to reside in an ocean found underneath the earth.

GIFTS FROM THE CRADLE OF CIVILIZATION

The Mesopotamian culture ended during 634 to 638 CE. This is when Arab armies took over the region. Over time, the palaces, canals, and homes crumbled into ruins. Desert sands slowly covered famous landmarks. Not until the nineteenth century did scientists discover this buried history.

We owe much to this area of the world. The Mesopotamians were the first to study the human body and experiment with medicines. They first used weights and measures based on a number system. Today we keep time the way they designed. They invented the wheel, and the world's oldest pottery came from them. We gaze at constellations in the sky named by the Babylonians.

They kept careful written records of their technologies and discoveries on clay tablets. Some clay tablets in museums are still not decoded. They wait for translations from future scientists. Maybe one day *you* will reveal those secrets.

This tablet with numerical signs dates back from between 3500 and 3300 BCE. Inventing a system of weights and measures was critical to preserving the medical prescriptions and trading records.

GLOSSARY

aqueduct An underground channel designed to move water to a distant source, usually by gravity.

ashipu A Mesopotamian healer who offered prayers to gods and demons as a treatment for illnesses.

Assyrian Someone who lived in Assyria, in northern Mesopotamia.

asu A Mesopotamian doctor who treated illnesses with herbal remedies.

axle The pole or bar that passes through a wheel's center so it turns.

Babylonian The culture that flourished in central-southern ancient Mesopotamia.

bronze A yellowish-brown metal made by combining copper and tin.

cast To pour melted metal into a mold and allow it to harden.

city-state An independent city with its own government, completely separate from nearby countries.

comet A small ball of ice and rock that moves around the sun in an elliptical orbit.

cuneiform The system of writing in ancient Mesopotamia using wedge-shaped marks on clay tablets.

irrigation A system to artificially water fields so crops can grow.

kiln A very hot oven used to bake and harden pottery or bricks.

millennium A period of one thousand years.

ore Rock that is mined for its useful material, such as a metal or coal.

Sumerian The first human civilization, found in southern Mesopotamia between the Tigris and the Euphrates Rivers.

ziggurat A rectangular terraced mound, often with a temple on top, built by ancient Assyrians and Babylonians.

FOR MORE INFORMATION

The British Museum on Mesopotamia
The British Museum
Great Russell Street
London, England
WC1B 3DG
Website: http://www.mesopotamia.co.uk/menu.html
This is an interactive website showing Mesopotamian warfare, astronomers, ziggurats, gods and demons, and Mesopotamian writing.

The Canadian Society for Mesopotamian Studies
c/o RIM Project
University of Toronto
4 Bancroft Avenue, 4th floor
Toronto, ON M5S 1C1
Canada
(416) 978-4531
Website: http://projects.chass.utoronto.ca/csms/main.html
Founded in 1980, this society examines the literature, culture, and history of ancient Mesopotamia.

NASA
NASA Headquarters
300 E. Street SW, Suite 5R30
Washington, DC 20546
(202) 358-0001
Website: http://www.sunearthday.nasa.gov/2006/locations/babylon.php
NASA (National Aeronautics and Space Administration) provides information about the ancient Babylonian eclipse forecasts and other astronomy subjects.

The Oriental Institute
University of Chicago
1155 East 58th Street
Chicago, IL 60637
(773) 702-9520
Website: http://oi.uchicago.edu/collections/highlights/highlights-collection-mesopotamia
The online portion of the university has links to research projects and collections of art and artifacts from ancient Mesopotamia.

WEBSITES

Because of the changing nature of Internet links, Rosen Publishing has developed an online list of websites related to the subject of this book. This site is updated regularly. Please use this link to access the list:

http://www.rosenlinks.com/SRFAC/mtech

FOR FURTHER READING

Bryson, Bernarda. *Gilgamesh*. Sacramento, CA: Pied Piper Press, 2012.

Charles River editors. *The Greatest Civilizations of Ancient Mesopotamia: The History and Legacy of the Sumerians, Babylonians, Hittites, and Assyrians*. Cambridge, MA: Charles River Press, 2015.

Feinstein, Stephen. *Discover Ancient Mesopotamia*. Berkeley Heights, NJ: Enslow Publishers, 2014.

Fullman, Joseph. *Eyewitness Books: Ancient Civilizations.* New York, NY: Dorling Kindersley Publishers, 2013.

Head, Tom. *Ancient Mesopotamia*. Minneapolis, MN: ABDO, 2015

Kriwaczek, Paul. *Babylon: Mesopotamia and the Birth of Civilization*. New York, NY: St. Martin's Griffin, 2012.

Lassieur, Allison. *Ancient Mesopotamia*. Jefferson City, MO: Scholastic Library Publishing, 2012.

Nardo, Don. *Life in Ancient Mesopotamia.* San Diego, CA: Reference Point Press, 2013.

Nardo, Don. *Mesopotamia* (Exploring the Ancient World*)*. Mankato MN: Compass Point Books, 2012.

Oakes, Lorna. *Hands-On History Mesopotamia: All About Ancient Assyria and Babylonia*. Houston, TX: Armadillo Press, 2013.

Woods, Michael. *Ancient Agricultural Technology: From Sickles to Plows* (Technology in Ancient Cultures). Minneapolis, MN: Twenty-First Century Books, 2011.

BIBLIOGRAPHY

Bradfield, Jinni. "The Invention of the Wheel." Antiquity Now, August 20, 2013. Retrieved January 22, 2016 (http://antiquitynow.org/2013/08/20/kids-blog-the-invention-of-the-wheel-how-the-ancient-sumerians-got-humanity-rollin/).

The British Museum. "Mesopotamia Writing." Retrieved January 22, 2016 (http://www.mesopotamia.co.uk/writing/home_set.html).

Dartmouth. "Copper: An Ancient Metal." November 18, 2010. Retrieved January 22, 2016 (http://www.dartmouth.edu/~toxmetal/toxic-metals/more-metals/copper-history.html).

Mark, Joshua J. "Health Care in Ancient Mesopotamia." Ancient History Encyclopedia, May 21, 2014. Retrieved January 22, 2016 (http://www.ancient.eu/article/687/).

Nardo, Don. *Ancient Mesopotamia*. Farmington Hills, MI: Lucent, 2004.

Oriental Institute Museum. "Warfare and Empire." Retrieved January 22, 2016 (http://mesopotamia.lib.uchicago.edu/mesopotamialife/article.php?theme=Warfare%20and%20Empire).

Samuels, Charlie. *Technology in Mesopotamia*. New York, NY: Gareth Stevens Publishing, 2014.

Scholl, Elizabeth. *Ancient Mesopotamia*. Hockessin, DE: Mitchell Lane Publishers, 2010.

Shuttleworth, Martyn. "Mesopotamian Astronomy." Explorable, October 10, 2010. Retrieved January 22, 2016 (https://explorable.com/mesopotamian-astronomy).

Teall, Emily K. "Medicine and Doctoring in Ancient Mesopotamia." *Grand Valley Journal of History*, Volume 3, Issue 1, October 2014. Retrieved January 22, 2016 (http://scholarworks.gvsu.edu/cgi/viewcontent.cgi?article=1056&context=gvjh).

Time Maps. "Civilization: Ancient Mesopotamia." 2015. Retrieved January 22, 2016 (http://www.timemaps.com/civilization/ancient-mesopotamia).

INDEX

A

aqueducts, 6
astrology, 32
astronomy, 4, 32, 40

B

boats, 28

C

calendar, 4, 32
canals, 6, 22, 24, 28
cities, building of, 24, 36
clothing, 10
construction materials, 20

E

Euphrates River, 4, 6, 8, 20, 24, 28

F

food production, 8

G

glass, 18
gods, 32, 34

H

healers, 34
houses, building of, 20, 22

I

irrigation, 6, 8, 24

M

mathematics, 30, 40
measures, 30, 40
medicine, 34, 40
Mesopotamia, location of, 4
metals and metalworking, 16, 18

P

plows, 8
pottery, 12, 40

S

scribes, 38
stone carving, 18

T

Tigris River, 4, 6, 8, 20, 24, 28
time, keeping, 32, 40
transportation, 14, 28

W

warfare, 36
weaving, 10
weights, 30, 40
wheels, 4, 14, 28, 36, 40
writing, development of, 4, 38, 40

Z

ziggurats, 26

ABOUT THE AUTHOR

Kristi Holl has written many nonfiction books on a variety of social studies and science topics as well as books for writers. Kristi has a degree in elementary education and is the author of fifty books, both fiction and nonfiction, for children and adults. She has a keen interest in the history of the area known as the cradle of civilization. She is especially interested in how writing was invented in ancient Mesopotamia. As much as she loves antiques and old methods, she is very glad that she doesn't have to write her books in cuneiform, making wedge shapes by poking reeds into wet clay. In her spare time, Kristi enjoys learning about other countries, both through travel and by visiting museums. She lives in San Antonio, Texas, with her husband and within minutes of her children and grandchildren.

PHOTO CREDITS

Cover, p. 1 Heritage Images/Hulton Archive/Getty Images; p. 3 Tolga Tezcan/Shutterstock.com; p. 5 © Zdenek Kahjzr/Alamy Stock Photo; p. 7 © Anjo Kan/Alamy Stock Photo; p. 9 © Cindy Hopkins/Alamy Stock Photo; pp. 11, 13, 41 DEA/A. Dagli Orti/De Agostini/Getty Images; p. 15 Werner Forman/Universal Images Group/Getty Images; pp. 17, 21 Science & Society Picture Library/Getty Images; p. 19 DEA/A. De Gregorio/De Agostini/Getty Images; p. 23, 39 DEA/G. Dagli Orti/De Agostini/Getty Images; p. 25 Essam Al-Sudani/AFP/Getty Images; p. 27 rasoulali/iStock/Thinkstock; p. 29 DEA/G. Nimatallah/De Agostini/Getty Images; pp. 31, 33 DEA Picture Library/De Agostini/Getty Images; p. 35 Photo © Zev Radovan/Bridgeman Images; p. 37 Print Collector/Hulton Archive/Getty Images; cover; p. 1 tower of babel graphic Santi0103/Shutterstock.com; back cover and interior pages background map Marzolino/Shutterstock.com; cover and interior pages background textures and patterns zffoto/Shutterstock.com, Elena Larina/Shutterstock.com, llaszlo/Shutterstock.com.

Designer: Michael Moy; Editor: Heather Moore Niver; Photo Researcher: Heather Moore Niver